DJ MACKBOOGALOO

SY-STEM-MIX

Youth Empowerment Edition

MACKBOOGALOO

First published by MACKBOOGALOO MEDIA 2026

First edition

This book was professionally typeset on Reedsy.
Find out more at reedsy.com

Contents

Introduction

WELCOME TO SY-STEM-MIX

A REVOLUTIONARY CREATIVE ECO-SYSTEM IS HERE!

What is SY-STEM-MIX

SY-STEM-MIX is a fun, safe, and organized way for young creators to make music together, built on real music-industry rules. It gives youth a structured environment to collaborate creatively without fear of being ignored, exploited, or left out.

Why it Exists

SY-STEM-MIX teaches how to remix, how to share ideas respectfully, how to stay organized, and most importantly, how ownership, credits, royalties, and financial literacy actually work.

Most young creators have never been taught how money moves in the music industry. SY-STEM-MIX finally gives them the clarity the industry never explains.

The Trap Young Artists must Avoid

For over half a century, major record labels have operated less like creative partners and more like predatory lenders, offering money upfront while taking ownership of an artist's masters, publishing, image, and future income.

Today, none of this is necessary. Self-publishing is simple, distribution is cheap, and young creators can release music without giving away their rights. SY-STEM-MIX exists to teach the next generation how to collaborate, organize, and build their careers with full ownership, financial awareness, and zero dependency on predatory systems.

The Revolutionary Breakthrough

SY-STEM-MIX contains one of the most important innovations in modern music education: The Song Composition Integrity Test.

This single rule solves a problem the entire music industry has struggled with for decades: what counts as songwriting and what counts as production.

Publishers argue about it. Producers argue about it. Courts argue about it.

SY-STEM-MIX ends the confusion with one clear, fair, youth-friendly standard.

This book introduces a system so simple and so accurate that it has the power to reshape how remix culture understands ownership, credits, royalties, and creative contribution.

SY-STEM-MIX is not just helpful, it is revolutionary.

The Visibility Law Breakthrough

SY-STEM-MIX contains another major discovery the music industry never taught: global visibility is created by metadata, not by platforms. Many young creators upload music to places like SoundCloud or Bandcamp and believe the world can find them, but these platforms were never designed to be global databases. Without identifiers, credits, and structured metadata, a creator can have thousands of plays and still be invisible everywhere else.

SY-STEM-MIX shows youth how to escape this trap. When you add ISRC, Google can see your track. When you add ISWC, PROs can see your composition. When you add UPC, your release enters the worldwide catalog. Metadata becomes the address that tells the world where your music lives. With the right identifiers, any upload can become globally visible, no matter where it starts.

This discovery is as revolutionary as the Song Composition Integrity Test because it gives young creators the power to bypass algorithm walls and closed ecosystems. It turns every remix into a visibility engine and every creator into their own global mapmaker. SY-STEM-MIX transforms metadata from a technical detail into a tool of worldwide reach, opening doors the old industry never explained.

What it gives Youth

SY-STEM-MIX restores fairness, structure, and confidence. It gives young creators a language to understand ownership, a system to protect their work, and a workflow that mirrors the real music business.

It also teaches youth how to assign fair royalty splits after the remix is complete, so credits and metadata stay accurate and legally consistent.

Most importantly, SY-STEM-MIX turns every remix into a Financial Literacy lesson. Youth learn how royalties work, how to track their income, how to build a catalog, and how creative assets generate long-term value.

SY-STEM-MIX protects young creators from the confusion, mistakes, and exploitation common in most remix communities.

Surviving the AI Music Age

The AI music age is flooding the world with machine-made songs faster than any human can create; but this gives young creators a unique advantage. AI can copy patterns, but it cannot copy purpose, identity, culture, or soul.

SY-STEM-MIX teaches youth to build their creative power around the one thing AI can never replicate: their human story.

Every artist is an archetype: a Mystic, a Rebel, a Creator, a Rags-to-Riches Hero, an Influencer, and more. Archetypes shape how artists express themselves and how audiences connect with them.

SY-STEM-MIX helps youth discover their archetype so they can market their music through identity, not algorithms.

In a world where AI can generate infinite content, identity and ownership matter more than ever.

How the System Works

SY-STEM-MIX is built on a decentralized-but-organized structure. Every member operates their own independent SY-STEM-MIX project; a personal creative hub where they control their stems, ideas, collaborators, and remix projects.

These individual hubs connect into a private, community-based network with shared rules and a unified workflow. The result is a system that feels open and creative on the inside, but remains protected, structured, and organized as a whole.

SY-STEM-MIX is future-proof; it works on any platform and adapts as technology evolves.

Final Vision Statement

SY-STEM-MIX is more than a workflow; it is a cultural shift. It gives young creators a safe structure to collaborate, a language to understand ownership, and a pathway to build their own catalogs with confidence.

It empowers youth with the financial literacy, creative independence, and legal clarity they need to build real value from their art.

By the end of this handbook, you will understand how to collaborate, protect your work, earn royalties, and build your own creative ecosystem.

In a world where remix culture is fast, informal, and often legally incorrect, SY-STEM-MIX stands as a bold, innovative, and revolutionary model that finally makes creativity fair for everyone.

IMPORTANT NOTE: SY-STEM-MIX is an educational guide designed to help

young creators learn how music collaboration, credits, and royalties work. It's not a legal document, and it doesn't replace professional advice.

I

Cultural Impact Is In The Mix

"SY-STEM-MIX is the structure. The creators are the engine. Financial literacy is the objective. Cultural impact is our legacy."

-DJ MACKBOOGALOO (The Human Beat-Maker)

1

What SY-STEM-MIX is

SY-STEM-MIX is a collaborative remix workflow designed for young artists, DJs, musicians, producers and music-oriented people with no direct musical experience. It gives creators a simple, safe, and organized way to work together while learning real-world music-industry skills.

It helps you:

-Work together as a team.

-Share ideas safely.

-Remix each other's music.

-Learn real music-industry skills.

-Understand credits and royalties.

-Stay organized while having fun.

In SY-STEM-MIX, members can upload:

-Original songs.

-Stems.

-A cappellas.

-Beats.

-Loops.

-Solos.

-Instrument parts.

-Ideas.

Any track can be remixed into many versions, like how one Jamaican Dancehall riddim can inspire dozens of songs featuring multiple recording artists.

SY-STEM-MIX fixes this by giving everyone:

-A clear workflow.

-Clear ownership rules.

-A safe, organized way to collaborate.

This structure is what makes SY-STEM-MIX succeed where other remix communities fail.

2

Initiate a SY-STEM-MIX group

Anyone can become an Organizer simply by stepping up and inviting their music peers into a SY-STEM-MIX group. The Organizer is the person who starts the ecosystem, helps new members understand the workflow, and gets everyone set up. From there, the Organizer can initiate remixes or allow their peers to initiate remixes, creating a shared creative space where everyone learns the system together. This handbook is the Organizer's guide for teaching the rules clearly and consistently.

SY-STEM-MIX works on any collaboration platform and will continue to work even as tools and technology change.

SY-STEM-MIX is designed as a decentralized-but-organized system, which means every member runs their own SY-STEM-MIX project. Each member becomes the gatekeeper of their own creative space, controlling their stems, ideas, collaborators, and remix projects. This structure gives everyone independence while still keeping the whole group connected through shared rules, shared workflow, and shared respect.

How SY-STEM-MIX roles work (Quick Summary):

-The Organizer starts the group. One person steps up, invites their peers, and teaches them how the system works.

-Anyone can become a Lead Remixer. Every member can start their own remix project at any time.

-You can let others remix your music without your input. Upload your stems, step back, and let your peers create freely.

-You can lead a remix project when you want to. As a Lead Remixer, you organize collaborators, guide the creative direction, and finalize the royalty splits.

-Everyone controls their own creative hub. Each member manages their own stems, ideas, collaborators, and remix projects.

Platform Notice:

SY-STEM-MIX is an independent educational system. It does not own your music, your rights, or your creative projects.

The SY-STEM-MIX method was originally developed using Boombox.io because that is the platform Mack personally uses and understands. However, this handbook is not affiliated with, sponsored by, or endorsed by Boombox.io or any other company.

SY-STEM-MIX does not depend on any specific platform. The workflow only requires basic collaboration features such as file sharing, project organization, feedback tools, and version tracking. These features exist across many cloud-based music-collaboration platforms, including Splice, BandLab, Soundtrap (Spotify), Audiomack Creators, and Soundation.

Because these platforms offer the same essential capabilities, the SY-STEM-MIX method can be used on any similar tool. The system is platform-independent, future-proof, and designed to adapt as technology evolves.

3

Organizer vs. Lead Remixer

SY-STEM-MIX works because everyone understands their role. There are only two leadership roles in the system, and both are simple: The Organizer & Lead Remixer.

THE ORGANIZER

The Organizer is the person who starts the SY-STEM-MIX group. They invite members, explain the rules, and help everyone get set up so the ecosystem runs smoothly.

What the Organizer does:

-Starts the group and builds the ecosystem.

-Teaches new members how the workflow works.

-Helps everyone get organized and ready to collaborate.

What the Organizer does not do:

-They do not control anyone's music.

-They do not approve or deny remixes.

-They do not decide royalty splits.

-They do not run every project.

The Organizer is the guide, not the boss.

THE LEAD REMIXER

The Lead Remixer is the person who starts a remix project. Every member can become a Lead Remixer at any time.

What the Lead Remixer does:

-Chooses collaborators.

-Guides the creative direction.

-Makes final decisions on the remix.

-Approves the release.

-Assigns the final Composition & Master splits.

-Ensures the metadata is accurate.

The Lead Remixer is the project leader for that specific remix.

The Key Difference:

-The Organizer starts the group. The Lead Remixer starts the remix.

-The Organizer runs the ecosystem. The Lead Remixer runs the project.

-The Organizer opens the creative space. The Lead Remixer leads the creative mission.

-The Organizer is the community builder. The Lead Remixer is the creative director.

Together, they keep SY-STEM-MIX fair, organized, and fun for everyone.

4

Creative Guidelines (Setting your boundaries)

SY-STEM-MIX is built to protect everyone's time and creativity. Before sharing stems or starting a remix, every member can set Creative Guidelines; simple rules about how their music can be used. If you don't have any guidelines, just say so. What matters is that everything is clear from the start. Be sure to document your guidelines, or non-guidelines, in writing so everyone is clear from the beginning.

YOUTH-FRIENDLY CREATIVE ROLES IN SY-STEM-MIX

To set good guidelines, it helps to understand the different types of collaborators you may work with.

A remix team may include:

-Beatmaker; creates drum patterns, grooves, and rhythmic foundations.

-Vocalist; performs the main vocal parts.

-Lyric writer; writes the words and themes.

-DJ; shapes energy, transitions, and performance flow.

-Producer; guides the creative direction and overall sound.

-Sound Engineer/Mixer; balances levels, EQ, and effects to shape the final mix.

-Visual artist; designs cover art, branding, and visual identity.

These roles help young creators understand that collaboration is not just musical, it's creative teamwork across multiple skills.

Examples of Creative Guidelines:

"Keep it clean, no explicit lyrics."

"No political or controversial themes."

"Please keep the original melody recognizable."

"Feel free to change the genre completely."

5

Remix Permissions & Approval Rules

SY-STEM-MIX is built to protect everyone's time and creativity.

SHARING STEMS IN SY-STEM-MIX

When you share stems in SY-STEM-MIX, you automatically agree that remixes may be released, as long as your Creative Guidelines are followed. This is LICENSING!

When you give someone permission to remix your song, you are licensing your music. Licensing simply means allowing someone to use something you own under your rules.

Thus, SY-STEM-MIX uses a royalty-only licensing model, meaning no upfront payments, no legal paperwork, and no attorneys unless you choose to involve them. All you need is permission, Creative Guidelines, and a fair split once the remix is complete.

Approval is automatic if:

-Your guidelines were respected.

-The remix team followed the workflow.

The Lead Remixer:

The person who starts/initiates the remix project is the Lead Remixer.

They have the final say on:

-Release decisions

-Artwork

-Mix and master changes

-Metadata

-Distribution timing

This keeps projects moving and prevents disagreements.

6

Remix Ownership (Who owns what?)

SY-STEM-MIX teaches real-world music-industry rules in a simple, easy-to-understand way. With SY-STEM-MIX, you always keep 100% ownership of any original musical material you contribute to a remix.

A remix can originate from any of the following creative sources:

-Musicians getting together to create a new recording of an existing song composition without adding a "new" song composition.

-Original songs, which are full tracks that you created.

-Stems, which are separated parts like drums, bass, keys, or vocals.

-A cappellas, which are vocals with no music underneath.

-Instrumentals, which are full music tracks with no vocals.

-Beats, which are drum patterns or rhythm tracks that form the backbone of a song.

-Loops, which are repeating musical patterns, usually 4- or 8-bar phrases.

-Solos, which are single-instrument or vocal performances like guitar lines, piano riffs, or horn melodies.

-Ideas, which are any small musical spark, like a quick melody, a rhythm you tap out, a voice note, or a rough sketch you haven't developed yet.

Song Composition is the "Song" itself, which includes:

-The melody.

-The lyrics.

-The chord progression.

-Any musical idea that can be sung, played, taught, or written down = Song Composition.

These elements define the identity of the song. With SY-STEM-MIX, the Song Composition is split equally among everyone who helped create the new Song Composition for the remix.

HOW SY-STEM-MIX DECIDES WHAT COUNTS AS "NEW" SONGWRITING

SY-STEM-MIX uses the "SONG COMPOSITION INTEGRITY TEST"; a simple rule that removes all confusion:

If you add a new part that changes the melody, lyrics, or chords, then it is new songwriting. If you add a new part and it does not change the melody, lyrics, or chords, then it is production.

If removing the new part breaks the song, meaning the song loses a core musical idea it depends on, then it is new songwriting. If removing the new part only removes a vibe, a texture, or an effect, then it is production.

This rule separates songwriting from production, which is the number one source of arguments in remix culture.

Gray area:

There is still a gray area, because music is emotional and some production choices feel important even when they do not change the melody, lyrics, or chords. A drum pattern, a bass movement, or a texture can feel iconic, but emotional impact alone does not make something songwriting. The system is not perfect because creators experience music differently, but the Song Composition Integrity Test brings us much closer to fairness. By focusing on whether a part changes the core musical ideas or whether the song still works without it, young creators gain a clear, simple way to protect themselves and avoid the misunderstandings that used to cause so many conflicts in remix culture.

WHY THE SONG COMPOSITION INTEGRITY TEST MATTERS (Real-World Examples)

Understanding the difference between SONG and SOUND isn't just important for young creators, it's something even major artists, producers, and courts have struggled with. Two famous copyright battles show how confusing things can get when people don't separate melody and lyrics from vibe, rhythm, and production. These cases help explain why SY-STEM-MIX uses the Song Composition Integrity Test to keep everything clear and fair.

Example 1: The "Blurred Lines" Lawsuit (2013–2018)

The Blurred Lines case became one of the most debated copyright rulings in modern music. Marvin Gaye's family claimed that Robin Thicke and Pharrell's hit copied the "feel" of Got to Give It Up. They didn't argue that the melody, lyrics, or chords were copied, only that the groove, percussion style, and overall vibe were similar.

A jury eventually ruled that Blurred Lines infringed on Gaye's composition, even though the core musical ideas were different. Many musicians were surprised because the decision treated production elements (the SOUND) as if they were composition elements (the SONG). This case shows how confusing things can get when the line between songwriting and production isn't clearly defined.

For young creators, the lesson is simple, even professionals and courts can disagree about what counts as songwriting. That's why SY-STEM-MIX uses the Song Composition Integrity Test, a clear rule that says melody, lyrics, and chords define the song, not the vibe or the groove.

In simple terms: even grown-ups in court get confused about music, which is why SY-STEM-MIX gives you one clear rule to keep everything fair.

Note: The same confusion that caused the Blurred Lines lawsuit also affected many remix deals in the 1990s. Rights holders sometimes gave remixers publishing credit even when the remixer only added drums, groove, or production elements, because they mistakenly treated SOUND as if it were SONG. This is the exact misunderstanding that led a court to rule that the "feel" of Got to Give It Up counted as songwriting. SY-STEM-MIX fixes this problem by drawing a clear line: only new melody, lyrics, chords, or musical ideas count as Song Composition; everything else is Master Recording. This prevents the kind of confusion that has caused legal disputes and inconsistent remix deals for decades.

Example 2: The Steely & Clevie "Dem Bow" Lawsuit (2023–Present)

Another major copyright battle involves Jamaican producers Steely & Clevie, who created the 1989 track Fish Market. They claim that over 1,800 Reggaeton songs (including hits by Daddy Yankee, Bad Bunny, and Luis Fonsi) copied or sampled elements of their track, especially the famous "Dem Bow" rhythm (Riddim) that became the backbone of Reggaeton.

The case is complicated because it raises some of the biggest unanswered questions in modern music:

-When does a rhythm become a protected musical idea?

-When does influence turn into copying?

-Can a drum pattern be copyrighted?

-What counts as sampling versus inspiration?

Different courts and judges interpret these issues in different ways, which is why the case has grown so large and so debated. It exposes how rhythm, style, and cultural influence can create legal confusion when there is no clear rule separating song from sound.

This is exactly the confusion SY-STEM-MIX is designed to solve. The system teaches that a rhythm is not songwriting unless it becomes a melodic theme you can sing or clearly identify as part of the song's identity. That single rule gives young creators a simple, fair way to understand something that even the global music industry still argues about. By drawing a bright line between rhythm as sound and melody as song, SY-STEM-MIX removes fear, removes guesswork, and gives creators the confidence to innovate without worrying about invisible legal traps.

In simple terms: rhythms can inspire whole genres, but only melodies define a song; and SY-STEM-MIX keeps that line easy for you to see.

- Why These Cases Matter for SY-STEM-MIX

Both lawsuits show the same problem. When people don't separate SONG from SOUND, everything becomes confusing, even in court. SY-STEM-MIX gives youth a clear rule that avoids this confusion:

If removing the new part changes the melody, lyrics, or chords, then it is songwriting. If the song still works without it, then it is production. This rule protects young creators, keeps collaborations fair, and prevents the misunderstandings that caused these famous cases.

-Court Decisions on Copyright Law

Courts work hard to interpret copyright law, but their decisions are not perfect or permanent. Legal rulings can be challenged, appealed, or reconsidered because different judges may see the same musical situation in different ways. A court decision reflects one interpretation of the law at a specific moment; not an absolute truth about how music works creatively. That's why SY-STEM-MIX focuses on clear, practical guidelines that help young creators understand ownership in a way that makes sense in real-world music situations.

SONG vs. SOUND (CREATIVE CLASSIFICATION)

If your contribution changes the SONG, you earn Composition. If it only changes the SOUND, you earn Master.

SONG = melody, lyrics, chords, musical themes.

If the remix changes the SONG, it is songwriting.

Note: Keep in mind that genre changes do not create new compositions unless they introduce new melody or chords.

SOUND = drums, percussion, bass groove, synths, effects, tempo, genre

If the remix changes the SOUND, it is production.

A QUICK SUMMARY OF COMPOSITION vs. MASTER (ROYALTY CATEGORIES)

Composition = *the SONG itself.*

This includes the melody, lyrics, chords, and any musical idea you can sing, play, or write down.

People who create these ideas earn songwriting (publishing) royalties.

Master = *the RECORDING people hear.*

This is the final audio file; the performance, production, mix, and sound.

People who help create the recording earn Master royalties, even if they didn't write the song.

SY-STEM-MIX teaches both sides (Song & Recording) clearly, so young creators always know who owns what. Again, if your contribution changes the SONG, you earn Composition. If it only changes the SOUND, you earn Master.

The Remix Legal Gray Area:

Most commercial dance remixes operate in a legal gray area, but this reality is rarely explained to the creators actually making the music.

Many remixers don't know the difference between songwriting and production, don't understand when a remix becomes a new composition, and aren't aware of what counts as protectable musical expression. They often assume "making the beat" is songwriting (it usually isn't), assume "changing the vibe" means they changed the composition (it doesn't), and assume "adding drums" creates ownership (it doesn't).

Copyright scholars and U.S. government reports describe remix law as unpredictable, widely misunderstood, and often handled informally rather than through proper licensing. Because unlicensed remixes are technically derivative works, many would face legal challenges if formally audited, not due to bad intentions, but because the industry has historically relied on informal norms instead of clear legal guidance.

Most remixes never face scrutiny simply because they stay small, disputes remain private, and creators often don't understand their rights well enough to challenge anything. Platforms like Boombox.io encourage early split decisions because it simplifies metadata entry, not because it reflects how the music industry actually works. As a result, many commercial dance remixes end up with incorrect splits, incorrect credits, incorrect ownership classifications, and metadata that would not hold up under professional review, but they fly under the radar because no one complains.

SY-STEM-MIX brings this overlooked truth into the open and teaches young creators what the dance world never emphasizes: how to understand ownership correctly, how to avoid common mistakes, and how to navigate remix culture with clarity instead of confusion. This is one of the core reasons SY-STEM-MIX is truly revolutionary.

In simple terms: the remix world is fun but messy, so SY-STEM-MIX gives you clarity so you don't lose credit, ownership, or money.

If a publisher, PRO, or attorney audited the average commercial dance remix, they would find:

-The splits are wrong.

-The credits are wrong.

-The ownership is wrong.

-The composition vs. master distinction is wrong.

-The remix is classified incorrectly.

-The metadata is legally inconsistent.

-The credits are wrong, they credit producers as songwriters.

But because the remix world is fast, informal, and hype-driven, nobody checks unless money starts flowing.

SY-STEM-MIX matters here because it is the first system that:

-Acknowledges the gray area.

-Explains it clearly.

-Fixes it with the Song Composition Integrity Test.

-Separates Song vs. Sound.

-Uses the Two-Stage Split System.

-Gives the Lead Remixer final authority.

-Prevents the exact problems that plague 90% of commercial dance remixes.

With SY-STEM-MIX you're solving a problem the entire commercial dance music industry quietly struggles with.

Royalty-Free vs. Exclusive Audio (The Content ID Trap)

One of the biggest hidden dangers for young creators today is the misunderstanding between royalty-free and exclusive audio. SY-STEM-MIX teaches ownership clearly, but modern platforms like YouTube, TikTok, Instagram, and Facebook add another layer of rules that creators must understand to protect their releases.

Many youth believe that using royalty-free samples from Splice, LANDR, Loopcloud, Cymatics, or other sample libraries means their music is automatically safe for monetization. But this is not true.

Royalty-free simply means you can use the sound legally without paying royalties. It does not mean you own the sound. It does not mean the sound is exclusive to you. And it does not mean you can fingerprint it through YouTube Content ID or TikTok's music library.

YouTube, TikTok, and Meta only allow "exclusive" audio to be fingerprinted. If a sample is available to thousands of creators, the platform cannot allow one person to claim ownership of it.

This is why distributors like RouteNote, DistroKid, CD Baby, and Amuse remove Content ID access when they detect:

-Splice loops.

-LANDR samples.

-Loopcloud samples.

-Cymatics packs.

-Royalty-free drum loops.

-Public domain audio.

-Sound effects.

-Ambience or nature sounds.

-AI-generated vocals or speech.

-Any non-exclusive audio.

Even if you used the sample legally, you cannot claim it as your own recording.

If a distributor or platform detects non-exclusive audio:

-YouTube Content ID is removed.

-TikTok Sounds is removed.

-Instagram/Facebook Music Library is removed.

-Monetization is blocked.

-Fingerprinting is disabled.

Your release still goes live on Spotify, Apple Music, and YouTube Music, but you cannot monetize or protect it through Content ID.

The SY-STEM-MIX Rule:

If a sound is not exclusive to you, you cannot claim ownership of it. If you cannot claim ownership of it, you cannot fingerprint it. If you cannot fingerprint it, you cannot monetize it through Content ID.

20 EXAMPLES THAT DO "NOT" CREATE A NEW SONG COMPOSITION:

These are production or performance changes only, the song still works without them.

-Changing drum style; switching from Rock drums to Latin Cumbia percussion changes the "feel" but not the composition.

-Adding synth pads; pads add atmosphere but no new musical idea.

-Changing the bassline groove; this is production, not songwriting, unless the bassline turns into a melodic hook.

Note: A bassline only counts as a melodic theme when it becomes a recognizable hook you can hum and identify the song by even without vocals.

-Changing the tempo; faster or slower does not change the composition.

-Changing the genre; turning a Rock song into Latin Cumbia or EDM does not create new composition.

-Adding percussion layers; congas, guache, maracas, shakers, etc. do not count as new songwriting.

-Recording new vocals; new performance, same composition.

-Adding vocal harmonies; harmonies do not create new composition unless they introduce a new melody.

-Adding FX and transitions; risers, sweeps, drops, and impacts are production only.

-Rearranging the structure; moving the chorus or extending the intro does not create new composition.

-Adding a new drum kit sound; changing from acoustic to electronic drums is production.

-Adding background textures; drones, noise beds, and ambience do not count as songwriting.

-Changing the key; transposing up or down does not create new composition.

-Changing the bass instrument; switching from bass guitar to synth bass is not songwriting.

-Adding ad-libs; they are performance unless they introduce a new melody.

-Adding a new beat pattern; unless it becomes a signature rhythmic theme, it is production.

-Adding a new intro soundscape; atmospheric intros do not count as composition.

-Adding a breakdown section; unless it introduces new melody or chords, it is arrangement only.

-Adding an instrument layer; extra guitars, synths, or percussion do not create new composition.

-Changing vocal effects; autotune, reverb, delay, and distortion are production choices.

These changes can make a remix sound completely different, but they do "not" change the song. They create a new Master Recording, but not a "new" Composition.

20 EXAMPLES THAT "DO" CREATE A "NEW" SONG COMPOSITION:

These are true songwriting changes; the song depends on them.

-Adding a new lead melody; a new melodic line is new songwriting.

-Adding a new vocal hook; a new singable hook becomes part of the song.

-Adding new lyrics; always creates new composition.

-Adding new chord progression and new harmony; creates a new composition.

-Adding a counter-melody, if it becomes part of the song's identity; it creates a new composition.

-Adding a new rhythmic hook; a rhythm that becomes a signature theme is songwriting.

-Adding a new instrumental theme; if it can be sung or taught, it's composition.

-Adding a new chorus melody; changing the chorus melody creates a new composition.

-Adding a new bridge section; a new musical section is new songwriting.

-Adding a new melodic bassline; if the bassline becomes a recognizable musical idea, it counts.

-Adding a new rap verse; new lyrics and flow create a new composition.

-Adding a new pre-chorus melody; a new section with new melody is songwriting.

-Adding a call-and-response hook; if it becomes part of the song, it counts.

-Adding a melodic percussion pattern; if percussion becomes a melodic theme, it is composition.

-Adding a solo that introduces a new theme; if the solo introduces a new melody, it counts.

-Adding new harmonic movement; new chords or modulations that change the song's identity create a new song composition.

-Adding a new refrain; a repeated melodic phrase is songwriting.

-Adding a new verse melody; changing the verse melody creates new composition.

-Adding an instrumental hook; if it becomes the signature of the remix, it counts.

-Adding a new melodic motif; a motif that can be sung or taught is composition.

These changes do alter the song itself. They create a new Song Composition, which is split equally among the remixers who contributed those musical ideas.

Side Note: *In many global music traditions, drums are not just rhythm; they are melody, language, and meaning. Yoruba talking drums (dundun, gangan) can imitate the tones of spoken Yoruba, carrying names, praise poetry, and full musical phrases. In Juju music and other West African styles, these drum lines function like melodic hooks, not background percussion.*

Modern genres follow the same pattern: Amapiano's log-drum basslines and Trap's 808 slides often behave like melodies, not just low-end impact. When these movements create a recognizable musical idea, they function as songwriting, not just production.

SY-STEM-MIX applies the Song Composition Integrity Test across all cultures and genres.

If a new part changes the melody, lyrics, or chords, it is songwriting. If it does not change those three things, it is production. If removing the part breaks the melody or the meaning of the song, then it is songwriting, even if the instrument is a drum or a bass. If removing the part only removes a vibe or a texture, then it is production.

This teaches young creators that not all "drums" or "basslines" are the same, and that global music systems often blur the line between rhythm and melody in ways Western copyright does not fully understand.

SY-STEM-MIX Golden Rule: If your contribution changes the SONG, you earn Composition. If it only changes the SOUND, you earn Master.

COPYRIGHT BASICS EVERY YOUNG CREATOR MUST KNOW

Copyright registration normally costs around $60 per song in the United States.

Copyright is one of the most important parts of protecting your music, but it's also the part young creators hear the least about. In SY-STEM-MIX, we make it simple: copyright is the legal proof that a song belongs to you. Without copyright, you can't collect money if someone steals your work, samples your track, or uses your music without permission.

You automatically own copyright the moment you create a song, but automatic ownership is not the same as legal protection. If someone takes your track and blows up with it, a court will ask for registration, not screenshots or timestamps. Registering your copyright with the U.S. Copyright Office gives you the power to prove ownership, stop infringement, and collect real damages if someone uses your music without permission.

SY-STEM-MIX teaches this because copyright is Financial Literacy. It's not just paperwork: it's your shield, your proof, and your paycheck. Copyright is the foundation of ownership, royalties, licensing, sampling, and long-term income.

The traditional music industry benefits when artists don't understand copyright, but SY-STEM-MIX exists to give youth clarity, power, and independence. When young creators understand how copyright works, they understand how to protect their art, how to earn from it, and how to build a catalog that truly belongs to them.

In simple terms: copyright is your proof of ownership; it protects your music and helps you get paid.

MORAL RIGHTS (INTERNATIONAL LAW, excluding the U.S.)

Outside the United States, creators have something called Moral Rights; special rights that protect the personal connection between an artist and their work. These rights exist in most of Europe, Latin America, Africa, Asia, and many parts of the world. Even if a creator sells their copyright or signs a contract, their Moral Rights usually stay with them for life.

The first Moral Right is the right of attribution, which means the creator has the legal right to be credited as the author of the work. No one can remove your name, replace your name, or pretend they created your music. This is why SY-STEM-MIX emphasizes proper credits and metadata; in many countries, failing to credit someone isn't just disrespectful, it's illegal.

The second Moral Right is the right to prevent distortion, meaning no one is allowed to change your work in a way that harms your artistic integrity. If someone remixes your song in a way that misrepresents you, twists your message, or damages your artistic identity, you can legally stop them. This matters for youth because remix culture moves fast, and not every remix is respectful.

The third Moral Right is the right to protect your reputation. If someone uses your music in a hateful, offensive, or harmful context, you can legally object. Even if you don't own the copyright anymore, your reputation is still protected. This is especially important for young creators who are still building their identity and public image.

The United States is one of the few countries where Moral Rights are extremely limited, especially for music. But SY-STEM-MIX is a global system, and young creators need to understand that their rights change depending on where they live and where their music travels. In many countries, Moral Rights last for the creator's entire lifetime, and sometimes even after death.

For global youth, this means your music is not just property; it is a reflection of your identity, your culture, and your reputation. Moral Rights protect that identity no matter who you collaborate with, no matter who remixes your work, and no matter where your music goes.

FORMING AN LLC (WHY IT MATTERS FOR YOUNG CREATORS)

As young creators grow, one of the smartest moves they can make is forming an LLC. LLCs exist worldwide under different names, but they all serve the same purpose: protecting creators by separating their personal life from their music business.

An LLC (Limited Liability Company) is not just a business structure; it's a shield. It protects your personal money, your personal belongings, and your future income from any legal problems connected to your music. If something goes wrong with a release, a contract, a sample, or a dispute, an LLC keeps the issue inside the business instead of touching your personal life.

For many youth, an LLC is also the first step toward becoming a real entrepreneur. It allows you to open a business bank account, receive payments professionally, sign agreements, and keep your music income separate from your personal finances. It also helps you look serious when working with studios, engineers, producers, and collaborators.

SY-STEM-MIX teaches this because ownership is not just creative, it's legal and financial. When you release music under an LLC, you protect yourself, you protect your catalog, and you protect your future. And when you assign your copyrights to your LLC, your music becomes a real business asset that can earn money for years.

An LLC is not required to make music, but it is one of the smartest long-term decisions a young creator can make. It turns your creativity into a protected business, and it gives you the confidence to collaborate, release, and grow without fear.

MUSIC AS INTELLECTUAL PROPERTY

Every song you create is more than art; it is intellectual property, and intellectual property is an asset. In the same way people own houses, cars, or businesses, creators own the rights to their music. These rights have real financial value. They can earn royalties, be licensed, be sold, be inherited, and continue generating income long after the song is finished.

Most young creators never hear this truth: your music is property. Not in a boring legal way, but in a powerful, life-changing way. When you write a melody, record a vocal, produce a beat, or create a remix that passes the Song Composition Integrity Test, you are building a catalog of assets that can grow in value over time.

This is why SY-STEM-MIX teaches ownership so strongly. When youth understand that their music is intellectual property, they stop thinking like hobbyists and start thinking like creators who own something valuable. And when you assign your copyrights to your LLC, your music becomes a protected business asset; something that can earn money, be licensed, or even be passed down to your family.

Music is not just creativity; it is property, value, and wealth.

Every remix, every idea, every composition you contribute becomes part of your creative portfolio; a catalog that can grow, earn, and support you for years, and pass on to your children as an inheritance.

SAMPLING LAW

Sampling is one of the most powerful tools in modern music, but it is also one of the most misunderstood. A sample is any piece of someone else's recording that you copy into your own track; even if it's short, even if it's edited, even if it's unrecognizable to most people. Legally, a sample is still someone else's property, and using it without permission can create serious problems for a young creator.

In music law, sampling requires two different permissions, because every song has two different copyrights. The first is the Master Recording, which is the actual audio file you hear. The second is the Song Composition, which is the melody, lyrics, chords, and musical ideas underneath the recording.

To legally sample someone else's music, you must clear both sides:

-Master Clearance gives you permission to use the original audio recording.

-Publishing Clearance gives you permission to use the underlying songwriting.

If you only clear one side, the sample is still illegal. If you clear neither, the sample is definitely illegal. And if your remix or beat becomes successful, the rights-holders can demand money, block your release, or even take ownership of your song. This is why SY-STEM-MIX teaches youth to be extremely careful with samples — especially samples pulled from YouTube, old records, TikTok, or other people's beats.

When you don't clear a sample, the consequences depend on how big the song becomes. If the track stays small, no one may notice. But if it grows, the rights-holders can demand all the royalties, demand ownership of your master, demand ownership of your composition, force your distributor to remove the song, file a copyright claim or take legal action.

This is why the safest approach for young creators is to use royalty-free samples, public-domain material, original recordings, or stems shared inside SY-STEM-MIX.

Sampling is different from interpolation, which is when you re-record or recreate someone else's melody, hook, or lyrics instead of copying their audio.

Interpolations do not require master clearance because you're not using the original recording; but they still require publishing clearance, because you are using someone else's songwriting. This is why interpolations often require permission, splits, and credit, even if you performed everything yourself.

SY-STEM-MIX teaches this because sampling law is one of the most confusing areas in music. Many young creators assume that changing the pitch, speeding up the audio, adding effects, or using only a tiny piece makes a sample "safe." Legally, it doesn't. A sample is a sample, even if it's chopped beyond recognition. Understanding this early protects youth from losing their songs, their royalties, or their creative momentum later.

LICENSING BASICS

Licensing is the part of music law that decides who can use a song, how they can use it, and how the creators get paid. Every time music appears in a movie, a remix, a TikTok video, a commercial, a video game, or even a cover song on Spotify, someone had to get the right license. SY-STEM-MIX teaches youth the creative side of collaboration, but understanding licensing gives them the power to protect their work and earn money from it.

The first type is the mechanical license, which is required whenever someone reproduces or distributes a song you wrote. This includes streaming, CDs, downloads, and covers. If someone records a cover of your song, they owe you mechanical royalties. If you cover someone else's song, you owe them the same. Mechanical licenses protect the Song Composition, not the recording.

The second type is the sync license, which is needed when music is paired with video: movies, YouTube, TikTok, TV, ads, games, trailers, and more. Sync licenses are powerful because they can pay well and expose your music to new audiences. A sync license always requires permission from the publisher (the songwriting side), and often from the master owner too.

The third type is the master use license, which gives someone permission to use the actual audio recording. If a filmmaker wants to use your exact track, not a cover, not a remake, they need a master use license. This protects the Master Recording, not the composition.

The fourth type is the sampling license, which is required when you copy any piece of someone else's recording into your own track. Sampling requires two permissions: one for the master and one for the composition. If you don't clear both, the sample is illegal, even if it's short, chopped, reversed, or heavily edited.

The fifth type is the remix license, which is permission to create a new version of someone else's song. A remix license is different from a sampling license because you're not just copying audio; you're creating a new derivative work. In the commercial world, remix licenses are negotiated directly with the rights-holders, and they often include rules about credits, splits, and distribution.

Licensing may sound complicated, but the idea is simple: music is intellectual property, and licenses are the rules for how that property can be used. When young creators understand licensing, they understand how to protect their work, how to collaborate safely, and how to earn money from the opportunities that come their way.

HOW ROYALTIES FLOW

Most young creators think royalties are one big payment, but the truth is that music money comes from different systems, each paying for a different part of the song. SY-STEM-MIX teaches ownership and splits, but understanding how royalties actually move through the industry gives youth real financial power. When you know how the money flows, you know how to protect it.

The first system is the Performing Rights Organizations, or PROs. These include ASCAP, BMI, SESAC, SOCAN, PRS, and others around the world. PROs pay songwriters and publishers whenever a song is performed publicly: streaming, radio, concerts, TV, restaurants, TikTok, and more. PROs do not pay producers, engineers, or performers. They only pay the people who own the Song Composition.

The second system is the music distributor, like DistroKid, TuneCore, CD Baby, UnitedMasters, or RouteNote. Distributors pay the people who own the Master Recording; the actual audio file. This includes producers, remixers, performers, engineers, and anyone listed in the master split. Distributors pay for streams, downloads, and sales.

The third system is mechanical royalties, which pay songwriters whenever their composition is reproduced: streaming, downloads, CDs, vinyl, and covers. In the U.S., mechanical royalties are collected by The MLC (Mechanical Licensing Collective). Outside the U.S., they are collected by different agencies. Mechanical royalties always go to the songwriters and publishers, not the performers.

The fourth system is streaming royalties, which are split into two parts: one part goes to the master owners (through the distributor), and the other part goes to the songwriters (through PROs and mechanical royalties). Streaming does not pay much per play, but it pays forever, which is why owning your catalog matters.

The fifth system is YouTube Content ID, which pays when your music appears in YouTube videos, even user-generated content. Content ID pays the master owners, not the songwriters, unless the publisher also participates. This is why metadata and accurate splits matter: if your name is wrong, the money goes to someone else.

The sixth system is SoundExchange, which pays performers and master owners when their music is played on non-interactive digital radio, like Pandora Radio, SiriusXM, iHeartRadio, and more.

SoundExchange pays three groups:

-The featured performer.

-The non-featured performers.

-The master owner.

SoundExchange does not pay songwriters. It only pays for the recording. Explore more: SoundExchange royalties

When youth understand these systems, they understand why SY-STEM-MIX separates Song vs Sound, why metadata must be correct, and why splits must be assigned after the remix is complete. Royalties are not magic; they are the result of a global network of organizations, each paying for a different part of the music. When young creators learn how the money flows, they learn how to build long-term value from their art.

WORK FOR HIRE

"Work for Hire" is one of the most dangerous phrases in the music industry, especially for young creators. It sounds harmless, but legally it means that the person doing the work does not own what they created. The person who pays for the work becomes the legal author, the copyright owner, and the royalty owner; even if they didn't write a note or record a sound.

In a Work for Hire agreement, the creator gives up all rights to the Song Composition and the Master Recording. That means no royalties, no ownership, no control, no credit disputes, and no future income. Once you sign a Work for Hire contract, the music is no longer yours; not now, not later, not ever.

This is why Work for Hire is so dangerous for youth. A young producer might make a beat, a vocalist might record a hook, or a remixer might create a full arrangement, and if they sign a Work for Hire agreement, they legally walk away with nothing. Even if the song becomes a global hit, the creator has no claim to royalties, no right to negotiate splits, and no ability to challenge how the music is used.

Work for Hire also affects credit. Because the hiring party becomes the legal author, they can choose whether or not to credit the actual creator. In many countries outside the U.S., this conflicts with Moral Rights, but in the U.S., Work for Hire overrides almost everything.

SY-STEM-MIX teaches youth to avoid Work for Hire agreements unless they fully understand what they are giving up. There are rare situations where Work for Hire makes sense, like when a creator is being paid a high fee for a job they don't need to own; but for young artists building a catalog, Work for Hire can erase years of creative value.

Understanding Work for Hire helps youth protect their music, their royalties, and their future. When you know what the phrase means, you know when to walk away, when to negotiate, and when to insist on keeping your rights.

COVERS AND INTERPOLATIONS

Understanding the difference between a cover and an interpolation is essential for every young creator. These two concepts determine whether you need permission, whether you owe publishing splits, and whether your remix is legally safe.

Covers:

A cover is when you perform or record your own version of an existing song without changing the songwriting. A cover keeps the original: Melody, Lyrics, Chords and Structure.

A cover is a new recording, not a new composition, which means, you do not need permission, you must pay mechanical royalties, you cannot change the composition, a cover does not create new publishing splits.

Interpolations:

An interpolation is when you use or recreate part of someone else's songwriting inside your new song. This includes re-singing someone's melody, rewriting their lyrics, recreating their hook, borrowing their chord progression in a recognizable way.

Interpolations change the composition, so they require permission, publishing clearance, songwriting credit, and royalty splits.

Interpolations always trigger the Song Composition Integrity Test.

Understanding the difference between a cover and an interpolation is essential because covers do not change the composition, while interpolations do. This is why SY-STEM-MIX teaches youth to separate SONG (composition) from SOUND (recording). When young creators learn this distinction early, they avoid legal mistakes, protect their ownership, and ensure every remix is credited fairly and correctly.

HOW A SOUND ENGINEER CAN EARN MASTER ROYALTIES & SONG COMPOSITION ROYALTIES

Most young creators can't afford expensive studio sessions, but they can afford to build relationships; and SY-STEM-MIX shows them how to turn those relationships into fair business.

Instead of paying high hourly fees, youth can invite a Sound Engineer into their creative ecosystem and compensate them through Master royalties or, when their creative input shapes the melody or musical idea, through Song Composition royalties as well. This transforms the engineer from a service provider into a collaborator, giving youth access to professional quality while keeping cash in their pockets. It also teaches them that a Sound Engineer's creative contributions can pass the Song Composition Integrity Test, and when that happens, royalties are the fairest form of payment.

SY-STEM-MIX brings this to light because the traditional industry hides these options, but youth deserve to know that collaboration, ownership, and royalty-based partnerships are not only possible, they are genius business moves that keep their music careers sustainable.

MASTER RECORDING IS THE FINAL RECORDED SONG FILE

A Master is the actual recording of the song; the audio file you hear.

In SY-STEM-MIX, the Master royalties are split equally among everyone who helped create the remix audio recording, regardless of whether they contributed songwriting. The only exception is the Lead Remixer, who earns an extra 5% bonus for guiding the project.

For example: A Lead Remixer might bring in collaborators who add drums, play instruments, record vocals, mix the track, or help shape the overall sound.

If a collaborator stops communicating or fails to follow through on their commitments, the Lead Remixer may remove them from the project; however, any meaningful work completed before removal still earns its share of Master royalties. This royalty structure ensures that everyone who contributes to the sound of the remix is recognized, respected, and rewarded.

HOW SY-STEM-MIX SOLVES THE DYNAMIC RANGE vs. LOUDNESS WAR

The music industry has battled for decades over dynamic range and loudness. Some engineers prefer clean, open, dynamic mixes that breathe; others push tracks louder so they hit harder in clubs, playlists, and DJ sets. This "loudness war" creates tension because one version of a song can't satisfy every listener, every platform, or every creative vision. And because the loudness-mastering wars dominated modern music for so long, an entire generation of youth has grown up hearing songs with almost no dynamic range; never realizing that music was once allowed to breathe, rise, and hit with natural impact.

SY-STEM-MIX solves this problem by allowing multiple Master recordings to exist for the same remix. Different sound engineers can create different versions: one with wide dynamic range, another with higher loudness for DJ performance, and even a third version optimized for streaming. Each version is still considered a valid Master under the same remix project, and all contributors keep their royalty splits exactly the same.

THE MIX MATTERS MORE THAN MASTERING (LEAD REMIXER ROLE)

There is a long-standing myth that mastering engineers are magical geniuses who can fix anything. In reality, the most important part of a great-sounding record is the mixdown. If the mix is clean, balanced, and slamming, the mastering engineer's job becomes simple: small EQ moves, light compression, and final loudness adjustments. Mastering can polish a great mix, but it cannot rescue a weak one.

This is why the Lead Remixer must oversee the mixdown process.

The Lead Remixer is responsible for making sure the remix sounds strong before it ever reaches a mastering engineer. That means checking levels, approving sound choices, ensuring clarity, and guiding collaborators toward a mix that already hits hard. A strong mix gives every mastering engineer a solid foundation to work from, and prevents the team from relying on mastering to "fix" problems that should have been solved earlier.

From a real music-business perspective, this approach is completely accurate:

-The mix determines 80-90% of the final sound.

-Mastering engineers often make tiny EQ adjustments (1–2 dB).

-Mastering cannot fix a bad mix.

-Producers (Lead Remixers) traditionally oversee the mix.

-Mastering is the final polish, not the creative rebuild.

When the mix is strong, different mastering engineers can create multiple Master versions (dynamic, loud, streaming-optimized, or DJ-ready) all without changing the creative identity of the remix. SY-STEM-MIX teaches young creators a professional truth. The mix does the heavy lifting, and mastering adds the final shine. The Lead Remixer protects this process by ensuring the remix is built on a strong, intentional mix that every version of the Master can rely on.

Online mastering tools can also be part of the SY-STEM-MIX workflow, but only when their limits are understood. These services use automated algorithms to analyze the mix and apply broad EQ curves, compression, stereo widening, and loudness adjustments based on preset profiles. They can enhance a mix that is already clean and well-balanced, but they cannot make artistic decisions, understand creative intent, or solve deeper problems like clashing frequencies, muddy low-end, harsh vocals, or poor arrangement choices.

Online mastering tools don't "fix" a mix; they interpret it. If the mix is strong, the algorithm enhances it; if the mix is weak, the algorithm exaggerates the weaknesses. This is why the Lead Remixer must ensure the mix is already hitting hard before any mastering happens. In SY-STEM-MIX, mastering (whether done by a human engineer or an online service) is the final polish, not the creative rebuild.

CREATIVITY COMES IN MANY FORMS

You can contribute as a Lead Remixer even if you don't play instruments; leadership, direction, taste, and creative vision also count.

Modern music producers are not defined by how many instruments they play, but by the decisions they make and the vision they bring to a project.

Many young producers today start with nothing more than a laptop and a strong sense of rhythm, emotion, and style; those skills are just as important as traditional musical training.

Legendary producer Rick Rubin is the perfect example: he doesn't program drums, play guitar, or sing on most of the albums he produces, yet his leadership, taste, and ability to guide artists shape the entire sound. His work proves that choosing what stays, what goes, and what the song should feel like is real creative contribution.

Points are an old music-industry slang term meaning a percentage of the master recording royalties, with one point equaling one percent. They are traditionally given to a producer who provides creative direction and oversight of the final sound, similar to a Rick Rubin-type role rather than a beatmaker or composer, and they apply only to the master side of the recording. SY-STEM-MIX replaces this confusing slang with clear master percentage splits based on actual creative contribution, removing the politics and ambiguity that often surround points in traditional industry deals.

In SY-STEM-MIX, those same skills are recognized and rewarded. A Lead Remixer earns Master royalties not because they play every instrument, but because they guide the creative direction, hold the vision, and help the team reach the best version of the remix.

THE LEAD REMIXER (ROLE DEFINITION)

The Lead Remixer role exists to keep projects moving, prevent arguments, and ensure every remix gets finished.

The Lead Remixer is the person who initiates the remix project and is responsible for organizing collaborators, guiding the creative direction, and finalizing the metadata. This leadership role gives the remix a single point of clarity so the project stays organized and reaches completion.

LEAD REMIXER BONUS

Producers earn Master royalties because they help shape the recording itself; the sound, the direction, and the final version people hear.

Leadership, decision-making, and creative vision are real contributions, even when the producer doesn't write melody or lyrics. This is why, in SY-STEM-MIX, the Lead Remixer receives an extra 5% of the Master royalties in addition to their equal share.

The Lead Remixer guides the creative direction of the remix, makes the final decisions, keeps the project organized, and ensures the remix gets finished. They also have the authority to release and distribute the new Master Recording once it is complete.

This leadership is real work, and the Lead Remixer Bonus keeps SY-STEM-MIX fair, clear, and easy to understand. It rewards the person who carries the responsibility of shaping the final recording while still treating every contributor with equal respect on the creative team.

REAL-WORLD FINANCIAL LITERACY

Every remix teaches real-world financial literacy. You learn how royalties work, how to track your income, and how to build a catalog that can earn money over time.

SY-STEM-MIX also creates a very real opportunity to make money, because every finished remix becomes a royalty-earning piece of intellectual property that you own a share of.

7

Royalty Collection for Master and Song Composition

Understanding how royalties are collected is one of the most important Financial Literacy skills a young creator can learn. Most artists never receive the money they are owed; not because they aren't talented, but because they don't understand how the royalty system works. SY-STEM-MIX teaches the truth early, so young creators can protect their income for life.

1. **Two Royalty Worlds: Master vs. Song Composition**

A. **SONG COMPOSITION** (Publishing Royalties)

These royalties pay the people who wrote the song: melody, lyrics, chords.

These royalties are collected by PROs in the United States (ASCAP, BMI, SESAC).

You use publishing administrators in the United States, like Songtrust, Sentric, or Kobalt, to collect your global publishing royalties; the money that comes from the songwriting side (composition).

Mechanical Agencies, like The MLC, exist to collect and pay out United States mechanical royalties; the money owed to songwriters and publishers when music is streamed or downloaded. They only handle the composition.

The MLC (Mechanical Licensing Collective) is the organization that pays out the mechanical royalties earned from streams and downloads of your songs. These royalties belong to the composition, not the recording, and they are calculated using the information connected to your ISWC. Registering your songs with the MLC ensures that every time your music is streamed on major platforms, the mechanical portion of your publishing royalties is tracked and paid directly to you or your publishing entity. Distributors do not handle this, and performance organizations do not collect these royalties. The MLC exists to make sure songwriters and publishers receive the mechanical income they are owed. Inside SY-STEM-MIX, this completes the ownership system: your ISRC protects the recording, your ISWC identifies the composition, your UPC identifies the release, and the MLC ensures the composition gets paid its mechanical share.

Publishing royalties include:

-Performance royalties

Performance royalties are earned whenever a song is publicly performed or broadcast, including radio, television, live concerts, DJ sets, restaurants, clubs, and digital streaming platforms. These royalties belong entirely to the composition side, meaning they pay the people who wrote the melody, lyrics, or chords. Performing rights organizations track when music is played in public spaces and distribute payments to the writers and composers. SY-STEM-MIX teaches creators that performance royalties are simply payments for public use of the underlying song, separate from the master recording.

-Mechanical royalties

Mechanical royalties are earned when a song's composition is reproduced, whether through streaming, downloads, CDs, vinyl, or any digital format that duplicates the melody, lyrics, or chords. These royalties go to the songwriters and composers, not the producer or beatmaker unless they contributed to the composition. Mechanical royalties are often misunderstood because they involve reproduction of the song rather than public performance, but SY-STEM-MIX simplifies them by teaching that mechanicals are reproduction payments for the underlying composition.

-International publishing royalties

International publishing royalties are the global versions of performance and mechanical royalties, collected when a song is played, streamed, or reproduced outside the songwriter's home country. Different nations have different collection systems, so publishers and administrators often work with international partners to ensure writers receive their earnings worldwide. These royalties matter because songs frequently travel far beyond their origin, and SY-STEM-MIX teaches creators that publishing is a global system with multiple collection networks.

-Sync royalties

Sync royalties come from sync licensing, which is the permission needed to use a song together with visual media. This includes films, television shows, commercials, video games, trailers, YouTube videos, TikTok posts, and any format where audio and visuals play at the same time. A sync license covers the composition side, so the people who wrote the melody, lyrics, or chords must grant permission. If the actual recording is used, a second license called a master-use license is required from whoever owns the recording.

SY-STEM-MIX teaches creators that sync royalties are simply payments for pairing a song with visuals, and that composition rights and master rights must both be cleared. These royalties do not work like performance or mechanical royalties, because sync payments are split between the people who wrote the song and the people who own the master recording.

B. **MASTER RECORDING** (Sound Recording Royalties)

These royalties pay the people who created the recording: performers, producers, beatmakers, engineers, mixers, anyone who contributed to the sound.

In the United States, these royalties are collected by Music Distributors (DistroKid, TuneCore, UnitedMasters, CD Baby, RouteNote).

SoundExchange collects one category of U.S. neighboring-rights royalties: digital performance royalties earned when a recording is broadcast on non-interactive services like Pandora or SiriusXM, ensuring that featured performers, non-featured performers, and master owners are paid for those digital public performances. They are the master-side equivalent of PROs.

Outside the United States, neighboring-rights agencies pay performers and master owners when recordings are played on radio, TV, clubs, and public venues. These agencies exist in countries like the U.K. (PPL), Canada (Re:Sound), and Germany (GVL).

YouTube Content ID systems automatically detect your recording in videos across YouTube in the United States and abroad, allowing the master owner to earn monetization royalties worldwide whenever their audio is used in user-generated content.

Master royalties include:

-Streaming and download revenue

-Digital performance royalties

-YouTube monetization

-International neighboring-rights royalties

These royalties only pay the people who contributed to the recording of the song.

WHY TWO ROYALTY SYSTEMS MATTER

These two royalty systems, SONG COMPOSITION (Publishing Royalties) and MASTER RECORDING (Sound Recording Royalties), do NOT overlap. You can earn from one, both, or neither, depending on your role.

For example:

-A songwriter earns publishing royalties even if they never step into the studio.

-A performer earns master royalties even if they didn't write the song.

-A producer may earn master royalties but not publishing royalties, unless they contributed to the composition.

This is why SY-STEM-MIX separates SONG from SOUND so clearly.

GLOBAL ROYALTY BYPASS FOR UNSTABLE MARKETS

In many developing music markets, royalty collection systems can be unreliable, underfunded, or affected by corruption, which makes it difficult for independent producers to receive fair payments. SY-STEM-MIX teaches creators to bypass unstable local structures entirely by using global tools that pay directly. Release your music through international distributors, register your compositions with trusted global PROs such as ASCAP, BMI, or Songtrust, and rely on platforms like YouTube Content ID, Spotify, TikTok, Bandcamp, and Patreon so revenue flows straight to you without local interference. Focus on worldwide streaming, direct-to-fan income, and micro-sync licensing instead of depending on local gatekeepers. This approach keeps your earnings clean, protects your rights, and connects your career to the global market rather than to systems that may not function reliably.

8

Surviving the AI Music Age

The AI music age is here, and it is flooding the world with machine-made songs at a speed no human can match; but that is exactly why young creators now have the greatest advantage in history.

Storytelling is embedded in our DNA; it is the oldest technology we possess. Long before computers, long before record labels, long before the entertainment industry existed, humans survived, taught, healed, and connected through story. Disney knows this. Hollywood knows this. Every empire built on imagination knows this.

SY-STEM-MIX teaches youth to embrace their human story, their identity, their culture, and to market their music through narrative, not noise. AI can generate patterns, but it cannot generate purpose. It can imitate style, but it cannot imitate soul.

Music as Promotion, Legacy as Wealth (The Human Artist Strategy)

In today's music world, streaming is no longer the main source of income for most artists. A million streams might pay a few thousand dollars, and young creators often feel discouraged when they realize how hard it is to earn real money from Spotify, Apple Music, or YouTube alone.

SY-STEM-MIX teaches a different way to think about music in the modern age. Music is not just a product... it is promotion!

Streaming platforms are global billboards. Every song you release is a digital flyer that promotes:

-your identity.

-your story.

-your brand.

-your live shows.

-your physical products.

-your workshops.

-your DJ sets.

-your creative services.

Music becomes the engine that drives attention, not the only place where money is made.

Human artists earn real, immediate money from:

-DJ gigs.

-live performances.

-workshops.

-teaching.

-events.

-merch.

-physical products.

-community building.

-cultural leadership.

These are things AI cannot replace. These are things that require a human presence, a human story, and a human identity.

Streaming is slow money. Shows and services are fast money.

SY-STEM-MIX teaches youth to use both.

Even though streaming pays slowly, your music catalog becomes a future asset; every song you release becomes:

-part of your legacy.

-part of your identity.

-part of your story.

-part of your long-term value.

A catalog grows in worth over time, especially when:

-you perform.

-you build a following.

-you teach.

-you collaborate.

-you stay consistent.

-you stay human.

AI can generate infinite songs, but it cannot generate your life, your culture, or your journey. Your catalog becomes a record of your existence; a creative fingerprint no machine can copy.

AI can make music, copy patterns and imitate styles, but AI cannot:

-perform on stage

-DJ a room.

-teach a workshop.

-shake a hand.

-build a community.

-inspire a crowd.

-tell a human story.

This is why SY-STEM-MIX teaches youth to think like creators, not just producers. Your music is the doorway. Your humanity is the value. Your catalog is the legacy.

This legacy strategy gives young creators the confidence to build a career that is:

-financially smart.

-creatively fulfilling.

-future-proof.

-human-centered.

-rooted in ownership.

In the AI age, your story is your superpower; and your catalog is the proof you were here.

THE HERO'S JOURNEY

Joseph Campbell discovered that myths, prophecies, and stories from around the world, stories that survived thousands of years, all follow the same fundamental structure called the MonoMyth, or the Hero's Journey. A hero leaves the ordinary world, enters a realm of challenge and transformation, faces trials, gains wisdom, and returns with gifts for the community. This pattern is not just a storytelling formula; it is the blueprint of human evolution. It is encoded into our DNA. It is the inner map that guides every young artist, every creator, every visionary who steps into the unknown to discover who they are.

Hollywood builds every successful movie around the Hero's Journey because humans resonate with it at a subconscious level. We recognize ourselves in it. We feel the call to adventure, the fear of stepping out, the trials, the transformation, and the return. Most people ignore the call and repeat their karmic lessons over and over. But creators, real "creators", eventually answer it. They step into the unknown, confront their shadows, discover their sacred path, and return with something only they can bring. This is what makes your story as a music artist valuable in the AI age.

AI EXPOSED THE TRUTH

In a strange way, the rise of AI did us a favor. It exposed the truth the industry has tried to hide; we are not machines. We are humans with a story, a spirit, and a lived experience that no algorithm can replicate. AI forced the world to confront the difference between content and meaning, between sound and soul, between imitation and identity. It reminded us that creativity is not just data; it is consciousness!

We are connected to something deeper, the World "Wood" Web, the living intelligence of nature, culture, ancestry, rhythm, memory, and life itself. Trees communicate. Ecosystems communicate. Humans communicate. Music is part of that same natural intelligence. AI can copy the surface, but it cannot tap into the roots. It cannot feel the pulse of a community, the weight of a struggle, the joy of a victory, or the spirit of a culture. Machines can make music, but only humans can make meaning.

ARTIST ARCHETYPES (YOUR STORY IS YOUR MARKETING)

Every artist is an archetype!

Every archetype is a story!

Every story is a marketing strategy!

AI can copy sound, but it cannot copy identity.

Some common artist archetypes include:

-**The Mystic**; spiritual, symbolic, consciousness-driven.

-**The Rags-to-Riches Hero**; daily struggle, drama, victory.

-**The Influencer/Icon;** lifestyle, wealth, aesthetics.

-**The Rebel**; anti-industry, truth-teller.

-**The Sage**; teacher, philosopher.

-**The Warrior**; discipline, hustle, motivation.

-**The Lover**; intimacy, emotion, vulnerability.

-**The Creator**; behind-the-scenes craft and artistry.

-**The Trickster**; humor, chaos, unpredictability.

-**The Healer**; emotional restoration and safe spaces.

-**The Everyman**; relatable, humble, community-based.

-**The Royal**; mastery, excellence, prestige.

Your archetype determines your marketing, your visuals, your captions, your storytelling, your audience, and your brand. This is why one artist naturally markets as a Mystic, another as a Rags-to-Riches Hero, and another as an Influencer. None of them planned it. It is who they are.

Note: Some artists are a combination of two archetypes, yet one archetype is usually more dominant.

THE AI AGE FORCES ARTISTS TO BECOME MORE HUMAN

AI can copy your sound, your style, your voice, and your patterns. But AI cannot copy your story, your archetype, your soul, your lived experience, your consciousness, your myth, or your Hero's Journey. This is why the future belongs to artists who know who they are, know their archetype, know their story, know their purpose, know their culture, know their roots, and know their consciousness.

SY-STEM-MIX gives youth the tools to survive the AI age by teaching them the one thing AI can never replicate: Human Identity!

THE DEATH OF MONOCULTURE & THE NEW RULES OF THE MUSIC WORLD

For most of the 20th century, the music industry was built on a single idea: Monoculture! A small number of radio stations, TV networks, magazines, and record labels controlled what the entire world heard. One hit could dominate the planet because everyone was listening to the same channels. The industry was centralized, top-down, and gatekeeper-driven. But that world is gone. The monoculture has collapsed, and the AI age has accelerated its disappearance. The old rules no longer apply, and young artists must understand the new landscape if they want to survive.

Today, there is no single mainstream. There are millions of micro-cultures, each with their own tastes, their own heroes, their own sounds, and their own internal rules. TikTok has its own cultures. YouTube has its own cultures. Gaming communities have their own cultures. Dance communities have their own cultures. Even within genres, there are sub-tribes, sub-scenes, and niche ecosystems that operate independently of the traditional music industry.

Young artists are no longer competing for one giant audience. They are competing for attention inside thousands of small worlds; each with its own language, identity, and values. This is why identity, story, and archetype matter more than ever. People follow creators who reflect their world, not the world the industry tries to force on them.

SPOTIFY FAVORS OLD LEGACY ARTISTS

Streaming platforms like Spotify operate on a principle called Cumulative Advantage. This means that artists who already have streams, followers, and history continue to benefit from the momentum they built years ago.

Older artists with large catalogs gain more algorithmic support because:

-They have more songs.

-They have more listening history.

-They have more playlist placements.

-They have more data for the algorithm to trust.

-They have more "stickiness" with listeners.

This creates a feedback loop where older artists continue to rise while new artists struggle to break through. It is not personal. It is math. The algorithm rewards what it already knows.

AI intensifies this problem. AI-generated playlists, AI-curated recommendations, and AI-driven listening habits push listeners toward familiar music, not new voices. The system is designed to reinforce the past, not introduce the future.

This is why many young artists feel invisible. The platform is not built to help them rise, it is built to keep the machine running smoothly.

WHY THE OLD RULES NO LONGER WORK

In the monoculture era, you could "get discovered."

In the streaming era, you must "build your world."

In the monoculture era, one hit could change your life.

In the AI era, one hit disappears in 24 hours.

In the monoculture era, the industry chose the stars.

In the AI era, algorithms choose what is familiar.

The rules have changed.

The path has changed.

The strategy must change.

THE RISE OF MICRO-CULTURES

Because monoculture is dead, the future belongs to artists who build their own micro-culture, a small but loyal world where their identity, story, and archetype resonate deeply.

Micro-cultures are powerful because:

-They are self-sustaining.

-They grow through identity, not algorithms.

-They create long-term fans, not temporary listeners.

-They reward authenticity, not imitation.

-They allow young artists to bypass the algorithm entirely.

This is why SY-STEM-MIX matters. It teaches youth how to build community, identity, and creative ecosystems; not just songs.

HOW SY-STEM-MIX PREPARES YOUTH FOR THE NEW WORLD

SY-STEM-MIX gives young creators the tools to survive in a world where monoculture is gone and algorithms favor the past.

It teaches them how to:

-Build their own creative micro-culture.

-Develop a strong identity and archetype.

-Create stories that resonate with real people.

-Collaborate to amplify each other's reach.

-Release more music, more consistently, with more clarity.

-Own their work so their catalog grows in value over time.

In a world where older artists benefit from Cumulative Advantage, young artists must build Cumulative Identity, a growing story, a growing culture, and a growing presence that algorithms cannot ignore.

THE NEW MUSIC TRUTH

The monoculture is dead.

The algorithm favors the past.

The AI age rewards familiarity, not discovery.

The future belongs to artists who build their own world.

SY-STEM-MIX gives youth the structure, the clarity, and the creative power to build that world together.

9

Legal Safety Tips

WHY COPYRIGHT EXISTS

Copyright exists to protect creators. When someone writes a song, records a performance, or produces a beat, the law gives them ownership over that work. This ownership allows them to earn money, control how their work is used, and prevent others from copying or exploiting it without permission. Copyright isn't meant to block creativity; it's meant to make sure artists are respected and credited for what they create. Understanding this helps young creators avoid mistakes and operate with confidence inside the music world.

WHY SAMPLING IS COMPLICATED

Sampling is powerful, but it's also legally tricky.

When you sample, you are using two copyrighted things at the same time:

-The composition (melody, lyrics, chords)

-The master recording (the actual audio file)

Even a tiny sample can trigger copyright issues because the law protects both the musical idea and the recording itself. Some samples are obvious; others are hidden, chopped, reversed, or heavily processed, but they can still be copyrighted. This is why SY-STEM-MIX encourages creators to use samples responsibly and understand the difference between inspiration and copying.

WHAT FAIR USE REALLY MEANS

Fair use is one of the most misunderstood concepts in music.

Many young creators think fair use means:

"I only used 3 seconds, so it's fine."

"I changed the pitch, so it's legal."

"I'm not making money, so it doesn't matter."

None of these are true!

Fair use is a legal defense, not a permission slip. It applies mostly to:

-Commentary

-Criticism

-Education

-Parody

-News reporting

Music remixes almost never qualify. That doesn't mean remixing is bad, it just means creators need to understand the rules so they don't rely on myths or misinformation.

SAFE WAYS TO REMIX LEGALLY

SY-STEM-MIX teaches youth how to remix safely without risking copyright problems.

Here are the safest options:

-Royalty-free sample packs; use these freely as long as you follow the license.

-Public domain music; older works whose copyright has expired.

-Original recordings; sounds you create yourself.

-Creative Commons samples; only if the license allows remixing.

-Cleared samples; when you have explicit permission.

-Stems shared inside SY-STEM-MIX.

This is appropriate because the creators voluntarily provide them with the group understanding and best practices, that those stems are legally legitimate. SY-STEM-MIX depends on every member participating in good faith and only uploading sounds, samples, and recordings they have the right to share. SY-STEM-MIX is built on trust, respect, and responsibility, and that means no one should upload copyrighted stems they don't own or don't have permission to use. When everyone follows this guideline, the whole community stays safe, creative, and protected.

These options let young creators experiment, learn, and grow without stepping into legal danger.

WHY THIS CHAPTER REALLY MATTERS

SY-STEM-MIX is built to protect young creators. Understanding copyright, sampling, fair use, and safe remixing gives youth the clarity the music industry rarely provides. When creators know the rules, they can break boundaries creatively and legally, and build a catalog they can proudly own and share.

10

Why Record Labels often act as predatory lenders

For decades, major record labels have acted less like creative partners and more like predatory lenders. They offer money upfront, called an advance, but the moment an artist accepts it, the label takes ownership of the artist's masters, publishing, image, likeness, touring, merchandise, and future income. These deals are designed so the label always wins, even when the artist loses everything.

In today's world, where self-publishing and digital distribution are easy and affordable, young creators should avoid signing with a label unless they are truly desperate and fully understand the cost and how it will affect their future.

Since the early 2000s, record labels often use 360 deals, which allow them to take a percentage of everything an artist earns: music sales, streaming, concerts, merchandise, sponsorships, acting roles, brand deals, and even social-media income. These deals were created because labels realized they could no longer control music sales alone, so they expanded their reach into every part of an artist's life. A 360 deal is not partnership; it is ownership.

History is full of examples showing how dangerous these deals can be.

Prince famously wrote "SLAVE" on his face because Warner Bros. owned his name, his masters, and his creative output. He had to change his name to a symbol just to escape the contract.

Michael Jackson spent years in legal battles with Sony over ownership of his masters and publishing rights, fighting a system designed to trap artists in long-term dependency.

At Motown, the legendary Funk Brothers, the musicians who played on nearly every hit, received no royalties, even though they created the hit-making sound that defined a generation. They were paid like day-laborers while the label kept everything.

Chuck Berry, one of the architects of rock and roll, was routinely pressured into payola-driven publishing deals in the 1950s, where radio DJs and promoters demanded the majority of his songwriting royalties in exchange for airplay. On many songs he was forced to give up roughly two-thirds of the publishing, meaning the creator kept only a third while the gatekeepers took control of the money.

These stories are not accidents, they are the business model.

Labels invest money the way a bank does, but instead of charging interest, they take ownership of your intellectual property, often forever. They own your masters, your publishing, your image, and your future income streams. And if your music doesn't recoup the advance, you still owe them, but they keep the rights anyway.

Today, none of this is necessary!

Self-publishing is simple!

Distribution is cheap!

Anyone can start their own label, release their own music, and keep 100% ownership of their masters and publishing.

SY-STEM-MIX teaches young creators how to collaborate, organize, and release music without giving away their rights. In a world where the tools are finally in your hands, signing your ownership away to a predatory label is almost never worth the cost.

And while SY-STEM-MIX teaches young creators to avoid predatory contracts, it also shows that you can strike a business arrangement with a record label, but only if you already own your masters, control your publishing, and use the label strategically as a bank and a promotional machine, never as your owner.

11

SY-STEM-MIX Workflow (Step-by-Step Guide)

The SY-STEM-MIX workflow is the heart of the entire system.

It gives young creators a clear, simple, repeatable process for making remixes together without confusion, arguments, or chaos.

Every remix follows the same steps, so everyone always knows what to do next.

This chapter shows the exact order of a SY-STEM-MIX remix from start to finish.

Before remixes begin, start a SY-STEM-MIX group. This begins with one person stepping up to start the ecosystem. This person becomes the Organizer, whose role is simply to invite their music peers, explain the SY-STEM-MIX rules, help everyone understand the workflow, and encourage good-faith participation. The Organizer is not a boss; the job is to be the spark that gets the ecosystem going and ensures the group begins with clarity instead of confusion. Once the group is formed and everyone understands the rules, the Organizer can start remix projects or allow others to start them. After this point, the system becomes decentralized, and anyone can lead a remix.

Step 1: START A REMIX PROJECT (LEAD REMIXER INITIATES)

Every remix begins when someone decides to start one. That person becomes the Lead Remixer.

The Lead Remixer:

-Initiates a new project.

-Uploads the original stems or invites someone else to upload theirs.

-Sets the creative direction.

-Explains the vibe, genre, or idea.

-Invites collaborators.

This step creates the creative home base for the remix.

Step 2: UPLOAD STEMS & CREATIVE ASSETS

Members upload:

-Stems.

-Beats.

-A cappellas.

-Loops.

-Solos.

-Ideas.

-Instrument parts.

These become the building blocks of the remix.

Everyone must upload only stems they legally own or have permission to share, following the good-faith rules of SY-STEM-MIX.

Step 3: SET CREATIVE GUIDELINES

Before anyone starts creating, the Lead Remixer confirms the guidelines.

For example:

"What are the boundaries?"

"What is allowed?"

"What is not allowed?"

"Is the original melody required?"

"Is the genre flexible?"

"Are explicit lyrics allowed?"

If someone has no guidelines, they simply say so. Clear guidelines prevent confusion later.

Step 4: COLLABORATORS CREATE FREELY

Now the fun begins!

The team members:

-Add drums.

-Write new melodies.

-Record vocals.

-Add chords.

-Create hooks.

-Shape the sound.

-Build the arrangement.

Everyone contributes in their own way!

The Lead Remixer keeps the project organized and makes sure the remix stays on track.

Step 5: REVIEW CONTRIBUTIONS (SONG vs. SOUND)

Once the creative work is done, the Lead Remixer reviews:

-Which parts changed the Song Composition.

-Which parts changed only the Sound.

-Which collaborators added new musical ideas.

-Which collaborators contributed to the recording.

This is where the Song Composition Integrity Test is used.

This step ensures fairness and accuracy.

Step 6: FINALIZE THE MIX

The Lead Remixer oversees the mixdown:

-Balancing levels.

-Cleaning up frequencies.

-Approving sound choices.

-Making sure the remix hits hard.

A strong mix is the foundation of every Master Recording.

Step 7: CREATE MASTER VERSIONS

SY-STEM-MIX allows multiple Masters:

-Dynamic version.

-Loud DJ version.

-Streaming-optimized version.

All versions share the same royalty splits. This gives youth creative freedom without legal confusion.

Step 8: ASSIGN ROYALTY SPLITS (FINAL STEP)

This is the moment that makes SY-STEM-MIX revolutionary.

Splits are never set at the beginning. They are set after the remix is complete, based on what actually happened.

The Lead Remixer:

-Assigns Composition splits.

-Assigns Master splits.

-Adds the 5% Lead Remixer bonus.

-Enters accurate metadata.

-Confirms all contributions

This creates a single point of truth and prevents disputes.

Step 9: APPROVE RELEASE

Approval is automatic if:

-Creative Guidelines were followed.

-The workflow was respected.

The Lead Remixer makes the final decisions on:

-Artwork.

-Release timing.

-Distribution.

-Final metadata.

This keeps projects moving and prevents endless debates.

Step 10: RELEASE & CELEBRATE

The remix is released. Everyone earns their fair share of royalties. Everyone gets proper credit. Everyone learns real music-business skills.

SY-STEM-MIX turns every remix into:

-A creative win.

-A learning experience.

-A financial literacy lesson.

-A confidence-building moment.

This is how youth grow into real creators.

12

Crediting & Metadata

Metadata is the digital DNA of your remix. It determines who gets credit, who gets paid, and how your music is tracked across Spotify, Apple Music, YouTube, PROs, and global databases. If the metadata is wrong or incomplete, royalties may never reach the right people. SY-STEM-MIX teaches youth the full picture so they can protect their work like professionals.

REMIX TITLE FORMAT

All remixes must follow the standard industry format:

-Original Title (Remixer Name Remix)

This format is recognized by all major distributors and ensures your remix is correctly identified as a new Master Recording, not a new Song Composition unless the Song Composition Integrity Test says otherwise.

-Required Credits (People Who Must Be Listed)

A remix must always credit the creators of the original song and the creators of the remix.

This includes:

-Original Artist(s).

-Original Composer(s).

-Original Lyricist(s).

-Remix Producer(s).

-Remix Arranger(s).

-Remix Programmer(s).

-Remix Mixer(s).

-Mastering Engineer.

-Sound Engineer.

-Lead Remixer (always listed first).

These roles ensure that everyone who shaped the Song Composition or the Master Recording is properly recognized.

REQUIRED METADATA FIELDS (INDUSTRY-STANDARD)

These fields determine how your remix is tracked and how royalties flow, and these identifiers are essential for royalty collection through PROs, distributors, and global databases.

Listed:

-Release Year.

-Record Label or Independent Artist name.

-Publisher(s).

-PRO Affiliations (ASCAP, BMI, SESAC, etc.).

-Copyright Owner(s) of the Composition.

-Master Owner(s) of the Recording

-ISRC; identifies the recording.

When you acquire your own ISRC Registrant Code, you step into full label ownership. You now have the power to generate unlimited ISRCs for free, and each code becomes the permanent identity of your recording everywhere in the world. Always register your music using the ISRCs you create yourself, and do not allow distributors like RouteNote, DistroKid, or anyone else to assign one for you. Enter your ISRC manually during upload and keep a clean log of every code you generate. As long as the audio stays the same, the ISRC stays the same; even if you switch distributors or re-release the track. This protects your catalog, keeps your metadata consistent, and gives SY-STEM-MIX the professional backbone it needs to operate globally. Your ISRC is your ownership. Your UPC is just the container. For digital releases, free UPCs are fine, but your ISRCs are the foundation of your power.

-ISWC; identifies the composition.

The ISWC, the identification number for the composition itself, is assigned only after you register your song with the organization that manages your songwriting and publishing rights. You do not create your own ISWC, and music distributors are not involved in this process at all. Once you submit the title, writers, publishers, and ownership shares, the information is processed through the global publishing system and an ISWC is issued automatically. This number belongs to the composition, while your ISRC and UPC belong to the recording and release. Inside SY-STEM-MIX, understanding this separation is essential because it teaches creators that publishing operates on its own track, with its own identifiers, royalties, and protections.

-UPC/EAN; identifies the release.

If you are releasing digital-only music and have no plans to sell physical products like CDs or vinyl in retail stores, you can safely use the free UPC (EAN is the European version of a UPC) assigned by your distributor. Digital platforms like Spotify, Apple Music, Amazon, and TikTok do not require you to own a GS1 barcode, and they do not check who the UPC prefix belongs to. All they need is a valid, unique UPC to identify the release. This means you can accept a distributor-assigned UPC with no downside, no loss of ownership, and no impact on your royalties. Your ISRC is what defines your recording and protects your rights; the UPC is simply the container for the release. For digital distribution, a free distributor UPC works perfectly and keeps your workflow simple and cost-effective. But once you begin building a long-term catalog, the identity of your release becomes more important than the convenience of a free code. This is where the UPC Law of Identity begins.

There is a quiet rule in the global music system that most creators never learn until something breaks. Every release has an identity. Every identity has a number. That number is the UPC. It is the code that tells the world your release exists. It is the code that keeps your catalog together. It is the code that protects your momentum. In SY-STEM-MIX, this is called the UPC Law of Identity.

A UPC is not for fans. A UPC is not for listeners. A UPC is not for the public. A UPC is for the machines that run the music world. Spotify reads it. Apple Music reads it. YouTube Music reads it. Amazon Music reads it. Google reads it. Shazam reads it. PRO databases read it. The UPC is the release identity inside the global system. Without it, your release is invisible. With it, your release becomes part of the worldwide catalog.

For years, creators believed UPC was only for physical products. CDs had UPC. Vinyl had UPC. DVDs had UPC. That was the old world. In the digital world, UPC became the identity for every release, physical or not. A digital single needs a UPC. A digital album needs a UPC. A digital EP needs a UPC. The global system does not care if the release is physical or digital. It only cares that the release has an identity.

Every distributor can generate a UPC for you. It works. It gets your release into the global system. But this convenience has a hidden consequence. The UPC belongs to the distributor's numbering system, not yours. If the distributor ever shuts down, loses your catalog, removes your release, or changes its internal system, you cannot reuse that UPC when you re-upload your music elsewhere. You must upload your release again with a new UPC. The platforms treat this new upload as a different product. The public sees the new version starting from zero. Your streams do not transfer. Your playlist placements do not transfer. Your algorithm traction does not transfer. Your saves do not transfer. You lose future money because the momentum you built is tied to the old release identity.

This is why owning your UPC matters. When you assign your own UPC, you become the source of your release identity. Your albums and singles stay grouped correctly. Your artist page looks cleaner. Your catalog stays consistent even if you switch distributors. Your releases do not split into duplicates. Your metadata stays stable. The public never sees the UPC, but they feel the difference every time they search for your name. Your catalog feels organized. Your identity feels complete. Your momentum continues instead of resetting.

The public does not notice the UPC itself. They notice how your catalog behaves. They notice when your releases stay together. They notice when your artist page looks clean. They notice when your songs appear in recommendations. They notice when your catalog does not break. They notice when your music is easy to find. They notice when your identity feels stable. The UPC is invisible to them, but its effects shape everything they see.

Using your own UPC is not about showing off. It is about control. It is about stability. It is about protecting your momentum. It is about making sure your catalog survives distributor changes, platform migrations, and industry shifts. It is about building a long term identity instead of a temporary presence. It is the difference between being a creator and being a catalog owner.

This is the UPC Law of Identity. If you control the UPC, you control the release. If you control the release, you control the catalog. If you control the catalog, you control the future.

The Creator's Path to Ownership:

Every creator begins with what they have, and that is enough. When you're starting out, using free identifiers, free tools, and free publishing options is not a shortcut; it's a strategy. These early resources let you release your work, build momentum, and learn the system without spending money or slowing down your creativity. None of this affects your intellectual property; your ideas, your stories, and your music remain fully yours. The only limitation is how your work appears in global databases: your brand may not show yet, and your identity may sit behind a generic label. That's temporary. As you grow, you'll reach a point where owning your identifiers becomes part of owning your voice. That's when you shift from simply releasing work to building a catalog, from building a catalog to building a brand, and from building a brand to building an empire. SY-STEM-MIX is designed to guide that evolution; start free, grow strong, and claim your identity when you're ready to stand as the official publisher of your books and the official label of your music.

WHY METADATA MATTERS

Most young creators lose money not because they aren't talented, but because their metadata is incomplete, incorrect, missing, inconsistent, not matched to their PRO registration, or not matched to their distributor upload.

Metadata determines:

-Who gets paid.

-How much they get paid.

-Who owns what.

-How the remix is tracked.

-How platforms identify the song.

Metadata mistakes are one of the biggest hidden reasons artists lose royalties. When the information in your remix doesn't match your PRO registration, the system can't connect your song to your identity, and your royalties may never reach you. A misspelled name, a wrong ISRC, or splits that don't match what you registered can cause payments to get stuck, delayed, or sent to the wrong person entirely. Even small errors, like using a nickname instead of your legal name, forgetting a collaborator, or entering the wrong percentage, can break the royalty chain.

Without correct metadata, a remix can become unpayable, uncredited, unprotected, and legally inconsistent. SY-STEM-MIX fixes this by teaching youth the full metadata chain, not just the visible credits, so they understand that one typo can cost more money than any creative mistake ever will.

GLOBAL VISIBILITY AND THE CLOSED-ECOSYSTEM TRAP

There is a quiet truth in the music world that most creators never discover until it is too late. Visibility is not automatic. Visibility is not guaranteed. Visibility is not a reward for talent. Visibility is a function of metadata. This is the law that SY-STEM-MIX teaches.

For years, young creators believed that uploading music to any platform meant the world could find it. They thought SoundCloud meant global reach. They thought Bandcamp meant global reach. They thought Audiomack meant global reach. But these platforms were never designed to be global databases. They were designed to be communities. They were designed to be storefronts. They were designed to be scenes. They were not designed to be the worldwide map of your identity.

This is why a creator can have fifty thousand downloads on SoundCloud and still be invisible everywhere else. The music is real. The audience is real. The talent is real. But the metadata is missing. And without metadata, the global system cannot see you.

Metadata is the postal address of your music. It tells the digital world where your release belongs. It tells Spotify who you are. It tells Apple Music what the release is. It tells YouTube Music how to group your tracks. It tells Shazam how to identify your sound. It tells Google how to index your catalog. Just like a letter cannot reach the right house without an address, your music cannot reach the global system without metadata. The address must be complete. The address must be accurate. The address must exist.

SoundCloud is a closed ecosystem. Bandcamp is a closed ecosystem. Audiomack is a closed ecosystem. Mixcloud is a closed ecosystem. These platforms do not require ISRC, ISWC, UPC, PRO-matched credits, global identifiers, or AI-aligned keywords. They do not feed Google. They do not feed Spotify. They do not feed YouTube Music. They do not feed Shazam. They do not feed PRO databases. They do not feed the global fingerprinting systems that track ownership and identity.

So your music lives inside the platform, but never connects to the world outside it. You become visible in one city, invisible in the world. You become known in one scene, unknown in the global database. You become heard by the people who already know where to look, but unheard by the people who search for you.

This is the closed-ecosystem trap.

But SY-STEM-MIX reveals the escape. Any platform can become globally visible after you add the correct metadata. The platform does not open. You open it. The platform does not connect. You connect it. The platform does not speak to the world. Your identifiers speak for you.

When you add ISRC, Google can see your track. When you add ISWC, PROs can see your composition. When you add UPC, the release becomes part of the global catalog. When you add credits, the system knows who made the music. When you add AI-aligned keywords, the search engines understand the culture, the mood, the diaspora, the vibe. When you add proper descriptions and tags, your SoundCloud page becomes a beacon instead of a shadow.

Metadata is not decoration. Metadata is direction. Metadata is the address that tells the world where your music lives. Without the address, the world cannot find you. With the address, every platform becomes part of your global identity.

The Global Visibility Breakthrough:

SY-STEM-MIX reveals something the music industry never taught: global visibility is not controlled by platforms; it is controlled by metadata. This discovery is as revolutionary as the Song Composition Integrity Test because it exposes the hidden architecture of the digital music world. It shows youth that they can bypass algorithm walls, closed ecosystems, and platform limitations simply by mastering identifiers, credits, and metadata structure. This turns every young creator into their own global distributor, their own visibility engine, and their own mapmaker. SY-STEM-MIX transforms metadata from a technical detail into a power tool, giving youth the ability to make any upload visible worldwide, no matter where it starts.

This breakthrough has the potential to reshape remix culture, creator education, and digital music literacy across the world.

This is the SY-STEM-MIX Visibility Law. A platform is not globally visible. Your metadata makes it globally visible. A platform is not a map. Your identifiers draw the map. A platform is not a bridge. Your credits build the bridge.

Once you understand this, the world opens. The closed ecosystems become part of your global identity. The forgotten uploads become searchable. The invisible catalog becomes visible. The music you made years ago finally enters the world for the first time.

Visibility is not magic. Visibility is metadata. And once you add it, every platform becomes part of your global story.

PROFESSIONAL METADATA STANDARDS

For deeper guidance, creators in the United States can refer to trusted industry authorities: U.S. Copyright Office, ASCAP, BMI, SESAC and The Recording Academy's Credits & Metadata Guidelines. These organizations define the global standards for how music is credited and tracked.

METADATA IS A MACRO STRATEGY

Metadata is the digital DNA of our music!

In the pre-AI era, artists were guessing. They typed random keywords, hoped the algorithm would notice, and released songs into a blind system that could not see them.

AI changes everything because metadata is no longer guesswork. It becomes precision targeting.

AI can map keyword clusters, genre clusters, search patterns, regional listening habits, BPM trends, and cultural tags that humans cannot track.

This means your metadata can finally match how people actually search for music today.

Metadata will not replace any macro moves you are making in the entertainment business, but it will amplify them.

Your catalog is a city.

Metadata is the street signs.

Without street signs, people wander. With street signs, people arrive.

SY-STEM-MIX teaches youth that metadata is the foundation of ownership, payment, and visibility. When metadata is correct, royalties flow. When metadata is wrong, royalties disappear.

AI gives creators the ability to build metadata that works, and SY-STEM-MIX shows them how to use that power to protect their work like professionals.

13

SY-STEM-MIX and Digital Collaboration Tools

SY-STEM-MIX was originally designed using the Boombox.io platform, but the workflow works on any modern music-collaboration tool that lets creators share files, communicate, and stay organized. No matter which platform a group uses, the same core features are needed to run a remix smoothly.

These are:

-File Uploads; stems, beats, vocals, and ideas.

-Collaborators; add team members and assign roles or splits.

-Messaging; communicate clearly during the remix.

-Tasks; assign responsibilities and keep the project moving.

-Project Settings; add artwork, metadata, and final details.

SY-STEM-MIX works best when these tools are simple, organized, and easy for youth to use. Boombox.io provided the original structure for building the SY-STEM-MIX workflow, but the system is platform-independent and can be adapted to any collaboration app with similar features.

14

Creative Freedom

SY-STEM-MIX encourages experimentation!

A remix is your chance to reshape a track, flip its energy, and explore new creative directions:

-Change genres.

-Change BPM.

-Flip the vibe.

-Transform the track completely.

For example: Turn a fast Footwork dance track into a slow House groove, or turn a Rock song into a Latin Cumbia song.

WHY REMIXING HELPS YOUNG ARTISTS GROW

Remixing is not copying; it is creative transformation. A remix takes something that already exists and reshapes it into a new expression, a new emotion, or a new perspective. Remixing is a language and a form of storytelling, allowing young creators to communicate ideas, flip meanings, and express themselves through sound.

Remixing also teaches essential musical skills: structure, rhythm, energy, arrangement, and how different musical elements work together. Every remix becomes a hands-on lesson in creativity, problem-solving, and artistic identity. Young artists grow faster when they remix because they learn by doing: experimenting, listening, adjusting, and discovering their own style through transformation.

SY-STEM-MIX gives youth the freedom to explore these creative possibilities inside a safe, organized system where experimentation is encouraged and respected.

15

Confidentiality

SY-STEM-MIX works best in trusted groups where people respect each other and share responsibly.

All files shared in SY-STEM-MIX are private:

-Keep stems private; don't share stems or works-in-progress outside the remix group without permission.

-Protect private links; never forward download links, folder links, or project links to anyone outside the group.

-Keep unfinished work off the internet; don't post drafts, previews, or early versions publicly.

-Respect creative boundaries; honor each member's creative space, ideas, and works-in-progress.

-Keep conversations inside the group; group discussions, feedback, and planning stay private unless everyone agrees to share.

16

AI-Generated Content & Sampling

To keep releases safe:

-AI-generated stems must be disclosed.

-Risky or unclear samples may be removed.

-Contributors are responsible for any samples they introduce.

This protects the whole team from takedowns or copyright issues.

17

Questions & Support

If you ever feel stuck or unsure about something in SY-STEM-MIX, reach out to your Organizer, a more experienced Lead Remixer, or a trusted member of your group. SY-STEM-MIX is a community built on teamwork and growth, and everyone is here to help each other learn, create, and level up together.

18

Putting it all together

SY-STEM-MIX gives you clear rules:

-Creative Guidelines.

-Ownership rules.

-Legal safety.

-Song vs. Sound.

-The Composition Integrity Test.

These rules protect you and keep the team fair.

A simple workflow, every remix follows the same path:

-Organizer starts the ecosystem.

-Lead Remixer starts the project.

-Upload stems.

-Set guidelines.

-Create.

-Review contributions.

-Finalize the mix.

-Create Master versions.

-Assign splits.

-Approve release.

This structure keeps everything organized and moving.

FAIR ROYALTIES & REAL-WORLD SKILLS

SY-STEM-MIX teaches you:

-How to earn royalties.

-How to protect your work.

-How to collaborate.

-How to lead.

-How to finish projects.

-How to build a music catalog.

-Every remix becomes a real music-business lesson.

THE BIG PICTURE

SY-STEM-MIX is:

-A safe place to create.

-A fair way to collaborate.

-A clear system for ownership.

-A real path to earning royalties.

-A community where everyone can grow.

You now have everything you need to remix with confidence, clarity, and creativity.

19

Final Note

SY-STEM-MIX is built to help young creators collaborate with confidence, learn real industry skills, and develop healthy creative habits that last a lifetime. It encourages teamwork, respect, and responsibility while giving every member a clear pathway to ownership and opportunity. SY-STEM-MIX is more than a workflow; it's a new way for young creators to collaborate, learn, and build their future.

At its core, SY-STEM-MIX is a community-powered remix system built on fairness, creativity, teamwork, transparency, and respect. It's a safe place to grow as a young artist and a fun way to learn real music-industry skills while making great music with friends.

SY-STEM-MIX is not just a system, it's a CULTURAL SHIFT, a new creative language, and a future that young artists get to build together.

IMPLEMENTATION GUIDE

SY-STEM-MIX must always be the face of the movement, not the individuals behind it.

In any city, the system should be presented as a neutral creative protocol rather than a crew, faction, or rival group. This protects your partners because SY-STEM-MIX absorbs the attention, the credit, and the blame, keeping individuals safe and out of conflict.

Local performers and youth groups serve as cultural ambassadors, introducing SY-STEM-MIX through movement, creativity, and positive energy so the system feels beneficial rather than territorial.

The rollout must be framed as an opportunity that fits naturally into the existing creative culture, not something that tries to change or replace it.

SY-STEM-MIX helps artists collaborate more, earn more, and organize their music while staying true to who they already are. Creative Guidelines (whether PG-13, genre-specific, thematic, or stylistic) are personal boundaries set by each individual artist, not system-wide rules. SY-STEM-MIX simply provides the structure for artists to declare their own guidelines clearly so collaborators know exactly what is allowed when remixing their stems.

The system also makes one thing clear: we warn youth about predatory practices from major corporate labels, but SY-STEM-MIX does not get involved in local city music-business politics, disputes, or shady situations. The system stays neutral so the community stays safe.

Royalty-only licensing removes financial tension by eliminating upfront payments, contracts, lawyers, and negotiations, replacing them with simple permission, personal Creative Guidelines, and fair splits after the remix is complete.

SY-STEM-MIX involves no bosses, no gatekeepers, and no central authority. Every artist runs their own creative hub, and the system stays distributed so no single person controls the process or the community.

Communication must stay simple and transparent, with rules, splits, and permissions openly understood to avoid suspicion or misunderstanding.

SY-STEM-MIX must remain apolitical, non-religious, non-tribal, and non-territorial so it can operate safely in any environment without triggering local conflicts.

The system should take the credit when things go well and the blame when things go wrong, keeping your partners protected behind the neutrality of the protocol.

Finally, the rollout should begin quietly and grow organically: a few performers introduce the vibe, a few artists test the system, a few remixes are released, and the community adopts SY-STEM-MIX naturally as they see the benefits for themselves.

ADDENDUM: What SY-STEM-MIX doesn't cover

SY-STEM-MIX is a youth-level guide designed to teach the essential foundations of collaboration, ownership, and creative safety. It gives you everything you need right now to create music confidently, protect your ideas, understand your rights, and collect the royalties you're owed.

The deeper business layers of the music industry (running a publishing company, forming an LLC, negotiating sync deals, managing a catalog, or building a long-term brand) are real and powerful, but they belong to a later stage of your journey. You don't need any of that yet.

Once you've mastered the basics and built enough music to scale, those advanced topics will be waiting for you in the next level of independence.

20 Advanced Topics to explore:

-Owning Your ISRC Prefix; how registrant codes work and why they matter long-term.

-Owning Your UPC Prefix; how GS1 barcodes affect catalog identity and label credibility.

-Black-Box Royalty Systems; how unclaimed royalties are redistributed globally.

-Distributor Market Share Strategy; how distributors use your metadata to negotiate deals.

-Catalog Portability & Migration; how to switch distributors without losing streams.

-Metadata Sovereignty; how to control your catalog's digital identity at the label level.

-Building a Digital Resource Hub; creating QR-linked guides, worksheets, or tools for your future audience.

-Forming an LLC for Your Music; how to legally structure your music business.

-Assigning Copyright to Your Company; how to transfer ownership to your LLC.

-Publishing Administration Systems; how global publishing collection actually works.

-Mechanical Royalty Infrastructure; how mechanicals flow through DSPs and publishers.

-Neighboring Rights & Performer Royalties; how artists earn money outside the U.S.

-Work-for-Hire Contracts; when to use them and how they affect ownership.

-Master Use Licensing; how to license recordings for film, TV, and ads.

-Sync Licensing & Music Supervision; how placements work and how to pitch.

-Global PRO Registration; how to collect royalties in every territory.

-SoundExchange & Digital Performance Royalties; how non-interactive streaming pays artists.

-Catalog Valuation & Acquisition; how investors price and buy catalogs.

-Predictive Analytics in A&R; how data identifies rising artists before the industry notices.

-Long-Term Catalog Wealth Strategy; how to build a catalog that pays for life.

AUTHOR: MACKBOOGALOO

DJ MACKBOOGALOO (official website):

https://www.mackthehumanbeatmaker.com/

MACK is a prolific Chicago DJ, Producer, Writer, and coordinator of inter-tribal unity efforts, now residing in Miami.

In a brave new world of Artificial Intelligence, MACK counters this trend by representing a living organic archetype that is driven by a desire to understand the world and share that understanding (books, music, websites, social media, live streams, podcasts, etc.) with others, aiming to find truth & enlightenment. MACK explores & archives themes relating to Roots, Culture and Consciousness. MACK infuses traditional wisdom into modern dance music, creating an experience that educates, entertains and elevates. MACK is a human Beat-Maker!

https://linktr.ee/cooleymack

Update: An Urban Street Literature empire, the result of AI reinventing the printing press, is in the works; a fusion of Urban (Hip-Hop) Sci-Fi Fantasy, Financial Literacy (music & book printing), Indigenous Elder Teachings, etc. Updated bio coming soon with links.

DJ MACKBOOGALOO strongly advocates the need for Youth Culture to turn towards Roots & Culture. To encourage this call-to-action, he has authored the book "Roots, Culture & Consciousness".

https://www.amazon.com/dp/B0D9WD512Z

DJ MACKBOOGALOO has carved his own niche within the SoundCloud community due to his Global Bass, Champeta, Chicago House, Footwork and Hip-Hop beat-making skills; reaching the benchmark of 50,000 (total) MP3 downloads of his DJ tracks in April of 2020.

https://soundcloud.com/mackboogaloo

DJ MACKBOOGALOO is an Afro-Caribbean music producer. His brand is called "TASTE OF THE FROZEN TROPICS", inspired by the Afro-Colombian "Champeta" sound system culture.

https://afro-loops-travel-agency.bandcamp.com

https://champeta-ton.bandcamp.com

DJ MACKBOOGALOO is a member of CHAMPETA-TRONIX/AFRO-GOLPEZ (AFRO-CARIBBEAN Electronic Dance Beats) with DJ Loko Cua Cua Champetuo of El Ultimo Hit & Son Caribe (picos) in Santa Marta, Colombia.

https://champeta-tronix.bandcamp.com/

Update: DJ MACKBOOGALOO is now an official DJ member & ambassador of the AFRO-STRIKES POSSE in Nairobi, Kenya (Eastlands), a collective that supports the

MOTIVATED MINDSET DANCERS of Mathare through music-driven revenue and financial-literacy empowerment, while also championing the AFRO-GOLPEZ genre founded by CHAMPETA-TRONIX, creating a cultural bridge connecting Kenya to their Afro-Caribbean relatives in Santa Marta (Colombia) and Miami. Updated bio coming soon with links.

https://www.youtube.com/@MOTIVATED.MINDSET.DANCERS/videos

DJ MACK "BOOGIE" LOU aka DJ HOT "JAZZY" MACK also has a large archive of Americana music, which includes Rockabilly, 50s & 60s Country Western, Chicago "Boogie" Blues and Traditional New Orleans Jazz. His brand is called "AMERICANA STEW".

https://www.mixcloud.com/HONKYTONKTALES/

DJ COOLEY MACK (CRN) helped pioneer Hip-Hop culture in the Midwest and Chicago among others in the Chi-Rock Nation during the mid-1980s to early-1990s. His music career began in 1986 with the arrival of the Ensoniq Mirage keyboard, a revolutionary low-budget sampling device for its time.

https://soundcloud.com/mackboogaloo/sets/dj-cooley-mack-old-school-hip

Update: DJ COOLEY MACK is returning to his Hip-Hop roots with a new rap collective (posse) of mostly OG lyricists named WINDY CITY-STYLE ROCKERS. Ready to flow (blow wind) over any style, any beat, from any location. Updated bio coming soon with links.

DJ COOLEY MACK was also tapped into the underground House Music scene of the 1980s; not as a "House DJ"... but as a student of the craft. Whether soaking up the DJ sounds of the Hot Mix 5 (WBMX) on the radio, Farley Jackmaster Funk at the Rainbo Roller Center, Lil Louis at Medusa's, or Jamie Lust (3:26) at his basement parties, he never missed a beat.

https://chicagoloopsexpress.bandcamp.com/

DJ COOLEY MACK studied "sound engineering" at Columbia College (Chicago) and was mentored by his teacher Malcolm Chisholm of the legendary Chess Records and Record Row fame. After a brief encounter with DJ Wayne Williams, he initiated an internship for himself at Jive Records. While interning, he had the pleasure of interacting with Chicago's finest House Music producers, like Hula & K. Fingers, Mr. Lee, Cajmere, Lidell Townsell, Maurice Joshua and others.

MACK has been deeply rooted in grassroots community empowerment since high school, serving as a youth mentor, case manager, and cultural educator across Chicago, Los Angeles, Compton, Long Beach, St. Paul, Minneapolis, Des Moines, Miami, and surrounding cities. His work has always centered on uplifting young people, and his current focus, now in Nairobi (Kenya), is financial literacy for the youth involved within the entertainment industry; a mission supported by his upcoming book publications.

DJ MACKBOOGALOO was blessed to have encounters with indigenous traditional elders (medicine people) in 2013, which led him on a path to assist their inter-tribal unity efforts. He became greatly inspired by the spiritual teachings of Mad Bear Anderson (Iroquois) & Rolling Thunder (Cherokee), along with Ted Silverhand (Iroquois), leading him to write books on their legacy.

https://www.amazon.com/dp/B0DBTZRHDG

https://www.amazon.com/dp/B0DC3NFJGG

https://www.amazon.com/dp/B0DC4Q2TGJ

DJ MACKBOOGALOO has joined the Conscious Youth Global Movement (CYGM), founded by elder & mentor Bikbaye Inejnema, which is promoting the Conscious expression of Youth through the Arts. He serves as the website's admin and is a regular content provider.

https://linktr.ee/cygm

www.ingramcontent.com/pod-product-compliance
Lightning Source LLC
LaVergne TN
LVHW020234210926
848481LV00016B/2199